How We Clean Up a Park

by Robin Nelson

first step nonfiction

Lerner Publications Company · Minneapolis

The images in this book are used with the permission of: © Todd Strand/Independent Picture Service.

Front Cover: © Todd Strand/Independent Picture Service.

Main body text set in ITC Avant Garde Gothic Std Medium 21/25.
Typeface provided by Adobe Systems.

Lerner Publications Company
A division of Lerner Publishing Group, Inc.
241 First Avenue North
Minneapolis, MN 55401 USA

For reading levels and more information, look up this title at www.lernerbooks.com.

Library of Congress Cataloging-in-Publication Data

Nelson, Robin, 1971–
    How we clean up a park / by Robin Nelson.
        pages   cm. — (First step nonfiction – responsibility in action)
    Includes index.
    ISBN 978–1–4677–3637–4 (lib. bdg. : alk. paper)
    ISBN 978–1–4677–3647–3 (eBook)
    1. Parks—Juvenile literature. 2. Environmental protection—Juvenile literature. I. Title.
SB481.3.N45 2014
    363.6′8—dc23   2013027015

Manufactured in the United States of America
1 – BP – 12/31/13

Table of Contents

Project Time!

My class has a special
project.

We are cleaning up a park!

Getting Ready

First, we put on gloves.

We all get **garbage bags**.

Next, we split into groups.

Group 1 gathers by the big tree.

Group 2 gathers by the playground.

Then it's time to clean up!

Cleaning Up

We pick up all the **trash** we see.

We put it in our bags.

Adults help with broken glass.

Finally, we **sort** the trash.

We put cans in a bag for **recycling**.

We throw away the other
trash.

That's how we cleaned up
the park.

How would you do it?

Activity

Write a Story

Pretend that you are responsible for cleaning up a park with your friends. On a separate sheet of paper, write a story about the steps that you would take to do this job. Use at least three of the words shown on the opposite page to write your story.

Story Word List

first

next

then

last

before

after

finally

Fun Facts

- A park in Japan has the world's longest playground slide. It is more than 167 feet (51 meters) long!

- There's a park in Sweden with playground equipment that looks like fruit. You can slide down a giant banana or climb on the watermelon jungle gym.

- Ducks, geese, robins, and blackbirds are common birds in many parks. Which of these birds is your favorite?

Glossary

garbage bags – large plastic bags that hold trash

project – a big job

recycling – making something new out of something that has already been used

sort – to group similar things together and separate them from things that are different

trash – things that are no longer wanted

Index